T0160561

EARLY POEMS 1913 — 1918

VLADIMIR MAYAKOVSKY

Translated by Maria Enzensberger
With a foreword by Elaine Feinstein

POCKET POETS SERIES NO. 47

CITY LIGHTS BOOKS
SAN FRANCISCO

First U.K. edition published by The Redstone Press, London

Translation © 1987 by Maria Enzensberger; Foreword © by Elaine Feinstein

Book design: Julian Rothenstein with Maria Enzensberger
Cover design: Rex Ray

Library of Congress Cataloging in Publication Data

Mayakovsky, Vladimir, 1893–1930
      [Poems. English. Selections]
       Listen! : early poems / by Vladimir Mayakovsky ; translated from the Russian by Maria Enzensberger.
       p. cm. -- (Pocket poets series ; 47)
ISBN: 0-87286-255-0 :
  1. Mayakovsky, Vladimir, 1893–1930--Translations, English.
I. Enzensberger, Maria. II. Title.
  PG3476.M3A23 1991
  891.71'42--dc20

Vist our website: www.citylights.com

CITY LIGHTS BOOKS are edited by Lawrence Ferlinghetti and Nancy J. Peters and published at the City Lights Bookstore, 261 Columbus Avenue, San Francisco, CA 94133.

CONTENTS

POEMS

LIST OF ILLUSTRATIONS

FOREWORD

These early lyrics of Mayakovsky will surprise any reader who has formed an opinion of his genius largely through reading his epic verse. In Burlyuk's flat, in which there were only mattresses for chairs and boards for a table, Mayakovsky had only recently understood that he was a poet. The excitement is poignant; the violence of metaphor is used so affectionately; cabbage and pineapple booze, stars and spittle, underwear and ginger wigs are all so evidently part of the pleasure he takes in the richness of the streets of the city. And for all the playfulness, Mayakovsky himself is always aware of that reality. 'His boots have holes, very real oval-shaped holes', as his friend Viktor Shlovsky put it.

Most of these poems have not yet been translated in the West. These versions are unlikely to be bettered. Maria Enzensberger has caught the movement and shape as well as the sense of the poetry, and picks up delightful rhymes without sacrificing the ordinary order of speech. This is altogether a remarkable book.

ELAINE FEINSTEIN

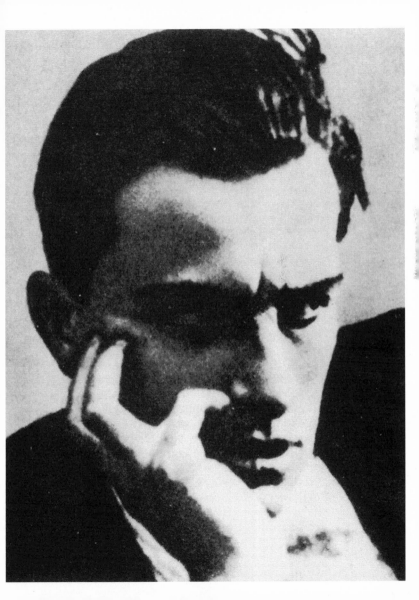

INTRODUCTION

The poetic career of Vladimir Mayakovsky started one night in 1912 on a Moscow boulevard. While taking a walk with David Burlyuk, a fellow student from art school, Mayakovsky recited a poem. He said it was by a friend of his.

'You wrote it yourself!' exclaimed Burlyuk. 'You are a genius!'

The next morning, as Mayakovsky later recalled in his autobiography, Burlyuk introduced him to someone as his genius friend, the famous poet Mayakovsky. 'Taking leave of me, he bellowed, "Now write or you will make me look a regular fool." So I had to write.'

David Burlyuk, himself a poet and a professional artist of some repute, has justly earned the reputation of being 'the father of Russian futurism'. A man of extraordinary organisational abilities, he was the driving force behind the activities of a group of avant-garde artists and poets, striving to promulgate the latest developments in European modernism on Russian soil: cubism in painting, futurism in poetry.

The group, which included Guro, Kruchenykh, Kamensky, Mayakovsky, Larionov, Goncharova, Tatlin and Malevich, published various illustrated literary miscellanies. They also held art exhibitions designed to shock conventional bourgeois tastes, issued strident manifestos and organised public debates and lectures vindicating the meaning and aspirations of the new art.

The Russian artists and poets, who had taken their cue from European movements, soon developed an indigenous style distinguished by its emphasis on illogicality and its affinity with Russian and Oriental primitivism. A synchronisation of the traditionally incompatible effects of the visual and verbal arts was the hallmark of the new movement in Russia. The very name, Cubo-Futurism, adopted by Moscow futurists in about 1913, attested to the close relationship between futurist poetry and cubist painting. In *Declaration of Word as Such* (1913), Kruchenykh described the process: 'Futurist painters like to use parts of the body, cross-sections; futurist poets use chopped words, half-words, and their whimsical, intricate combinations'.

The interplay of visual and verbal images is one of the most distinctive features of the early Mayakovsky. To understand his poetry, one must be able to 'see' it. Some of the poems included in this collection (I, WHAT ABOUT YOU?) can be described as painting with words: they read like poetic equivalents of cubist painting. The poem, TO SHOP SIGNS, is Mayakovsky's tribute to the primitive art of sign painting, which was so highly valued by futurists that an exhibition held by the Larionov group in 1913 included six works by members of The Second Workshop of Sign Painters. TO SHOP SIGNS first appeared in the miscellany, *Service-Book of the Three,* with illustrations by Mayakovsky and Tatlin.

Another typically futurist feature of the early Mayakovsky is his urbanism. Many of the poems before 1918 conjure up futuristic cityscapes. His urban imagery, which is often anthropomorphic, can be joltingly poignant and macabre:

Have you noticed
hanging in stony alleys
the striped face of condemned boredom

(Prologue to VLADIMIR MAYAKOVSKY: A TRAGEDY)

13

Доклад Владимира Маяковского:

(о живописи)

Бабушкам академий.

1) Вчерашния достижения и сегодняшний день
2) Группировка художественных сил в России
3) „Бубновый Валет" (переход на амплуа домашний"
4) Гончарова, Ларионов (ба-ба-бо лучизм)
5. Союз Молодежи
6) Знатные иностранцы
7) Матисс, Пикассо, Боччони.
8) Сказки о русских подражат.
9) Параллелизм в искусстве
10) Завтрашний день — футуризм!

The street's sunk like the nose of a syphilitic.

(AND YET . . .)

The voice of Mayakovsky's early poetry is anguished, suffering from profound loneliness and a lack of understanding and compassion. It is the anguish of the artist who cannot transcend his isolation or endure it any longer. There is a stark contrast between this persona and the better known Mayakovsky of later years: the poet of the revolution, the tribune of the people. But these early poems help to explain Mayakovsky's commitment to the revolution as well as his inability to resolve his problems through that commitment. Mayakovsky, the poet whose verses fell on the deaf ears of conventional and materialistic bourgeois audiences, is necessarily the hero of his first dramatic work, VLADIMIR MAYAKOVSKY: A TRAGEDY.

The revolution marked a turning point in Mayakovsky's poetry. For the first time he felt the possibility of joining in, of identifying himself with those who had overthrown the old order. As a poet, this meant the opportunity of reaching wider audiences, of speaking directly to the humble and downtrodden whom he had always regarded as his natural allies:

> But they won't blame me, won't bellow;
> Lining my road with flowers, they'll honour me
> like a prophet.
> Those, with sunken noses, know
> I am their poet.

(AND YET . . .)

The spirit and tone of Mayakovsky's poetry changed quite dramatically after the revolution. The present collection ends with the poem, CONCERN FOR HORSES, written in the Spring of 1918 while Mayakovsky was working on his three films, only one of which, *The Young Lady and the Hooligan,* has survived. In each of the three roles, which Mayakovsky wrote for himself and in which he starred, he recreated the same emotional persona, which had asserted itself throughout his pre-revolutionary poetry. Together with the last poem in this collection, these films mark a divide in Mayakovsky's career.

A few words on the problems of translating Mayakovsky.

Mayakovsky's is a poetry of metaphor and hyperbole. In addition to their symbolic meaning, his images have a concrete, palpable existence. To convey that, I have tried to produce as close and straightforward a translation of every word used in the original as I could. Similarly, I have tried to reproduce the rhythmic and sound structure of his verse: its broken staggered line, its assonances and alliterations, and, most importantly, its rhymes.

Mayakovsky often made alterations to his earlier poems. The versions I have worked from come from Volume I of his *Collected Works,* Moscow, 1955-61. The illustrations which appear in this volume have been selected from various futurist publications contemporaneous with the poems.

MARIA ENZENSBERGER

В. Маяковский

Рис. Чекрыгина и Л. Ш.

По мостовой моей души
      изъѣзженной
шаги помѣшанных
бьютъ жесткихъ фразъ пяты
    ГДѢ
       города
    повешены.
и в петлѣ облака застыли
      башенъ кривыя
    Выи
иду одинъ рыдать что пере-
         крестком
    .
    Распяты
    Города=
        ВЫЕ

I

Upon the cobbles

of my foot-clobbered soul,

the steps of loonies

twine their grinding rhymes.

Where the towns

are hung

and in the nooses of clouds

the crooked necks of towers

are wrung,

I start to cry

because

by the crossroads

the cops are crucified.

1 9 1 3

TO SHOP SIGNS

Read those iron books!
To the flute of the gilded letter
will sprout glamorous beetroot
and smoked sardines and salmon.

And once you turn joyous and pranky
among the constellations of 'Maggi',
a formidable undertaker
will sternly parade his sarcophagi.

And when, sullen and dismal,
the street has extinguished its lamp-posts,
fall in love in the starlight of taverns
with glittering poppies on teapots!

1913

WHAT ABOUT YOU?

I splintered the landscape of midday

by splashing colours from a tumbler.

I charted on a tray of aspic

the slanting cheekbones of Atlantis.

Upon the scales of an iron turbot,

I found ladies' lips, aloof.

And you,

        could you have played a nocturne

using a drainpipe for a flute?

1 9 1 3

23

24

from **VLADIMIR MAYAKOVSKY.**

A TRAGEDY:

PROLOGUE

You wouldn't understand

why,

cold as an ominous sneer,

I am carrying my soul to be slaughtered

for the dinner of impending years.

Rolling like an unwanted tear

from the unshaven cheek of the square,

I am probably the last poet.

Have you noticed

hanging in stony alleys

the striped face of condemned boredom

and, on the foamy necks

of galloping rivers,

the bridges have clasped iron fingers in mourning?

Мосты заломили железныя руки

И небо плачет безудержно и звонко

А у облачка гримаска на морщинке **ротика**

Как будто женщина ждала **А** ребенк

А Бог **ей** кинул кривого идіотика

Пухлыми па**ль**цами в **рыжих** волосиках

Солнце из**ласкало** вас с назойли- востью овода

В ваших *душах* выцелован раб

Я безстрашный ненависть к дневным **лучам** понес в веках

И с душой натянутой как **нервы** провода
Я **ц**арь ламп

The sky is crying,

inconsolably,

        loudly;

and a cloud's forced a smile

across its sombre wrinkles,

as if a woman had been expecting a child,

but God blessed her with a wretched little monster.

Stretching its plump hairy fingers,

the sun fondled you

with a gadfly's persistence:

a slave's been kissed into your hearts!

I am dauntless,

my dislike of sun-rays carrying through time.

With a soul strung as the nerves of a wire,

I am the lord of electric bulbs.

Come all to me,

those who loom through silence,

who groan

because the nooses at noon are too tight,

I'll show to you

with words simple as mooing

our new souls

roaring like the arched wrought-iron posts.

I'll only touch your foreheads with my fingers,

and you'll grow lips

for enormous kisses

and a tongue

native to all peoples.

And leaning upon my limping soul,

I'll stagger off towards my throne

with the holes of stars along its tatty dome.

Consoled,

in indolent clothes,

I'll relax on the soft bedding of genuine manure,

and gently kissing the knees of the railroad,

the wheel of a locomotive will embrace my throat.

MAYAKOVSKY

Ladies and gentlemen,

patch up my soul.

It could not leak if it were hollow.

Is a spit a blow? How am I to know?

A boulder-stone is as arid as I,

you've milked me dry.

Ladies and gentlemen,

                     come to the show:

this very moment,

                a great poet

will dance before you.

MAYAKOVSKY

**(raises his hand,
takes centre stage)**

Don't rub malice into hearts' ends!

You,

my children,

I'll teach

resolutely and eagerly:

all of you people

are mere bells

tinkling on God's headgear.

With a foot swollen by a quest

I have covered your continent

and many other lands.

In a domino

and a mask of darkness

I've been seeking her —

the soul

       that nobody's seen before,

longing to lay her healing flowers

on the blazing ulcer of my mouth.

(he pauses)

And again,

soaked in blood and sweat,

like a slave,

I am rocking my body with madness.

Incidentally,

I found her once — the soul.

She appeared in a florid dressing gown

and said:

'Please be seated. I've been waiting for you for a long time

Would you like a cup of tea?'

(he pauses)

I am a poet,

I've erased the difference

between the faces of friend and foe.

In every mortuary, I looked for sisters.

I kissed the leprous lacy sores.

And today,

on yellow bonfires,

having buried the tears of the seas,

I shall burn the disgrace of sisters

and grey-haired mothers' wrinkles.

Off the plates of licentious feasts,

we'll be gobbling your meat, carnal century!

(He moves to the side, softly)

Ladies and gentlemen,

haven't you heard

somewhere —

        I believe in Brazil —

there is one happy creature.

39

E P I L O G U E

I wrote all that about you,

poor rats.

Sadly, God's given me no breasts

or I'd suckle you like an anxious mare.

At the moment, I am somewhat drained,

not all there.

But then,

        who,

              where

has ever given such meteoric freedom

to thought?

          It's I

who poked a finger at the sky,

espied

        the sky's a pickpocket.

Sometimes I think

                        I am a Dutch cock

or

   indeed

            a Pskov[1] king,

but —

           all things considered —

                        I prefer my own name

Vladimir Mayakovsky.

1 9 1 3

---

[1] An old Russian town that never had a king.

TAKE IT!

In another hour, out of the foyer,

all your sizzling dripping will flow, man by man.

And I have revealed such hoards of verse before you,

I — squanderer and prodigal of priceless words.

Sir, I say, there's cabbage in your beard

left over from yesterday's meals.

Madam, hey, your make-up is smeared;

you stare like an oyster from the shells of things.

All of you, filthy, in galoshes or without,

will clamber onto the butterfly of the poet's heart;

the crowd'll go wild, get roused,

it will throw up its legs, the hundred-headed louse.

And what if today, I, coarse Vandal,

refuse to entertain you, still worse —

burst out laughing and spit into your faces,

I — squanderer and prodigal of priceless words.

1 9 1 3

Y O U !

You, wallowing in orgy after orgy,

owning a bathroom and a warm loo,

how do you feel learning about the awards of St Georgy[1]

from the papers in your morning room?

Do you know, insentient nonentities,

thinking only of how to fill your maw,

that this moment, the legs of Petrov the lieutenant

were ripped off by a bomb?

And what if he, brought for slaughter,

suddenly saw, unrepining,

how you, with your mouths oily,

lasciviously hum Severyanin[2]?

To give my life for the sake of you —

lips drivelling with lust?

I'd sooner serve pineapple booze

to the whores in Moscow bars.

1 9 1 5

[1] Military decoration
[2] Fashionable poet from the rival Ego-futurist camp

AND YET . . .

The street's sunk like the nose of a syphilitic.

The river is lust, trickling away with saliva.

Having cast off its underwear down to the last twig,

the garden is shamelessly basking in the summer.

I came out into a square.

       A scorched house

I put onto my head like a ginger wig.

People are afraid — out of my mouth,

an unuttered cry is wriggling its feet.

But they won't blame me, won't bellow.

Lining my road with flowers, they'll honour me like

        a prophet.

Those, with sunken noses, know

I am their poet.

I fear your last judgement no more than a throng.

Me alone, through blazing cities roaming,

prostitutes, like an idol, will carry along

and show to God as their atonement.

And God will start crying over my book:

these are not words — convulsions compressed into lumps.

He'll run through the sky, my poems in his hands,

and, spluttering, show them to his friends.

1 9 1 4

LISTEN!

Listen,

if stars are lit,

it means there is someone who needs it.

It means that someone wants them to be,

that someone deems those speckles of spit

                                     magnificent.

And overwrought,

in the swirls of afternoon dust,

he bursts in on God,

afraid he might be already late.

In tears,

he kisses God's sinewy hand

and begs him to guarantee

that there will definitely be a star.

He swears

he won't be able to stand

                                  that starless ordeal.

Later,

he wanders around, worried,

but outwardly calm.

And to someone else, he says:

'Now,

it's all right.

You are no longer afraid,

are you?'

Listen,

if stars are lit,

it means there is someone who needs it.

It means it is essential

that every evening

at least one star should ascend

over the crest of the building.

1 9 1 4

from **THE BACKBONE-FLUTE**

PROLOGUE

To all of you —

those I liked or like —

cherished as icons in the cave of my soul,

solemnly, I raise as a goblet of wine

the skull filled with my poetry.

I contemplate —

                so often —

ending my days

with the full stop of a bullet.

This evening,

                for all of you —

                        just in case —

I am giving a farewell concert.

Memory,

pack the brain's auditorium

with inexhaustible swarms of beloveds.

Spatter laughter from eye to eye,

sate the night with former weddings' glory.

Fill every soul with a jocular mood

so that this night is forgotten by no one.

Today, I shall play the flute —

my backbone.

1 9 1 5

Пусть не забудется любовь милая.

Я сегодня буду играть на флейте

На собственном позвоночнике.

CONCERN FOR HORSES

Hoofs sang,

stamping the ground:

'Grot,

Grand,

Grit,

Groomed.'

Ice-shod,

wind-hounded,

the street

skidded underfoot.

Suddenly,

a horse slumped on its croup.

At once,

all those drifters flared-trousered

gathered in force.

Laughter

spilled and spouted:

'A horse tumbled!

Look at the horse!'

The Kuznétsky[1] rumbled.

[1] Moscow street

Only I

didn't join my voice in the sneering.

I came nearer

        and saw

the eye of the horse . . .

The street, tipped over,

continued on its course . . .

I came nearer

        and saw

a large tear

        roll down the muzzle,

glisten,

        and disappear . . .

And some sort of fellow animal pain

splashed out of me

and flowed in whispering:

'Horse, please . . .

Horse, listen,

why should you think you are any worse?

Darling,

we are all

      essentially horses,

each and every one of us is something of a horse.'

Maybe

     the old one

         didn't need my comfort,

maybe

    my thought

        was too effete,

only the horse tried hard,

          neighed loud,

rose to its feet,

    and made a start.

Its tail playing

    in glittering coat,

it trotted indomitably toward its stall.

It suddenly felt

    it was still a colt

and life was definitely worth living again.

1 9 1 8

портрет строителя завершенного

K. Malevich: Portrait of a Builder completed 1913

ACKNOWLEDGEMENTS

I would like to thank all those who gave me their support and encouragement while I was working on these translations of Mayakovsky.

I am deeply grateful to Neal Ascherson who was the first to hear and commend my earliest attempts; to Maria Ascherson, Neal's daughter, Ruth Jarratt and Gessy Gathercole for going with me over my first translations and making some valuable suggestions; to Di Laurillard who became so enthusiastic about the poems that she arranged to have them professionally laid-out and typed. I want to thank Elizabeth Millar and Mary Mayer for their relentless questioning of my choice of words and the patience with which they read through many a different version of the same poem and Peter Mayer for his help with illustrations.

I am deeply indebted to Emma Tennant for her kind words of praise and encouragement. Elaine and Arnold Feinstein I shall never be able to thank enough for their interest in my work and help in launching the present edition. I want to thank Julian Rothenstein for the zeal and inventiveness with which he put this edition together.

Finally, I would like to remember the organisers and participants of the East Midlands Arts Film Weekend, Derby, January 1984, where I made a presentation on Mayakovsky and Cinema — the experience which set me off on the track of translating the early Mayakovsky.

MARIA ENZENSBERGER

BIOGRAPHICAL NOTE

Maria Enzensberger was born in Moscow, the daughter of a famous Soviet poet Margarita Aliger. She read English at Moscow University. Having married the German poet and essayist Hans Magnus Enzensberger, she left the Soviet Union in 1967 and lived in the United States, Cuba and Germany before coming to Britain in 1969. She made this country her permanent home while always maintaining close links with her native Russia. She taught Russian at the Universities of Essex, Sussex and Surrey before becoming one of the first women Fellows of King's College, Cambridge, 1972-1976. The subject of her research and various publications are the Russian avant-garde arts and literature of the first decades of this century. Maria Enzensberger has a special interest in cinema and is at present translating Eisenstein for the multi-volume edition of his writings prepared by the British Film Institute.